AF594216

JUMBO
JACK'S COOKBOOKS
AUDUBON MEDIA CORPORATION
301 BROADWAY • AUDUBON IA 50025
1-800-798-2635

WARNING!

The enclosed recipes are for purposes of entertainment only. The recipes and other instructions are not to be used in preparing food for human consumption. The writer and publisher disclaims any responsibility for the results of anyone foolish enough to do so.

IOWA'S ROADKILL COOKBOOK

by

Bruce Carlson

QUIXOTE PRESS
31798 K18S
Sioux City, Iowa 51109

* * * * * * * * * * *

QUIXOTE
PRESS
Bruce Carlson
31798 K18S
Sioux City, Iowa 51109

PRINTED
IN
U.S.A.

DEDICATION

This book is fondly dedicated to The Dean of Road Kill Cookery, Professor Emeritus Wm. H.A. Moser, University of Idaho, Iowa City, Ohio.

TABLE OF CONTENTS

FOREWORD

IOWA'S ROAD KILL COOKBOOK provides Iowa *Ventre Montanters* (French for "those who salvage animals that are Belly-Up") with a source of information about proper procedures and recipes.

The recipes in IOWA'S ROAD KILL COOKBOOK use, as the main ingredients, those feathered or hairy creatures who find their final resting places alone side of, or on, Iowa's highways.

Whatever one's gastronomic ambitions, IOWA'S ROAD KILL COOKBOOK provides a delightful evening of reading.

Inof Splist
Literary Review Office
Journal of the Party Line
Prilspe, Hungary

PREFACE

I made a remarkable discovery one evening while doing some calculations.

I discovered there was a large difference between the daily fatalities of various critters on Iowa highways and the number of those critters removed by scavangers such as crows and coyotes.

According to my calculations, the state's crows and coyotes would almost have to stand wing to shoulder to remove all those animals that have a meaningful relationship with an oil pan at 55 miles an hour every night.

So what happens to all those carcasses? What happens, I discovered, is that many of them end up in Iowa ovens. Tasty dishes using *Ventre Mortant* (French for Belly-Up) are being prepared in Iowa every day. This book compiles some of the recipes. The reader is urged to refer to page 1 about these.

CHAPTER I

The history and practice of the culinary arts has greatly neglected the art of *Ventre Montant* .

Ventre Montant is derived from the French and can be literally translated to "belly up". It refers to the art of preparing delicious and nutritionally sound meals from gamey; er, game animals that expired, as a result of tramatic accelerating due to vehicular impact. These are sometimes referred to as "road kills" or "road pizza."

By whatever name, the accomplished practioneer of *Ventre Montant* cookery can prepare dishes that delight the eye, nourish the body, and soothe the soul.

As with other speciality cooking, there are practices pecular to *Ventre Montant*. The neophyte *Ventre Montanter* will, on occasion, mistake a section of a steel radial for a turtle or a flattened oil filter for a pheasant.

With a practiced eye and a little diligence, this kind of an error can be avoided. A later section of this book will serve as a primer on techiniques for the identification of remains that are of uncertain orgin.

Another common mistake is the use of tools inadequate for the job. For example, very often the unskilled will use an aluminum scoop shovel to gather roadside remains. As one's palate develops, it soon becomes obvious that a plastic scoop is preferred. It is not only less apt to impart a metallic taste to the meat, but it also is less vulnerable to corrosion by the delicate fumes which often emanate from critters that have laid on hot concrete for a few days.

For those recipes calling for pressure cooking, it is necessary to use ½ inch gauge pots to develop the heat and pressure necessary to entice those delicate bouquets and flavors from some dishes. A later chapter would have offered some detailed instructions on how to adapt a Bessmer Converter to a suitable pressure cooker, except I lost interest.

PIT BBQed RED MOUND

This recipe gets its name from those deer that get hit along the highway so badly that they don't really look like deer anymore, just mounds of red stuff.

Slide the whole mess over onto an old car hood or piece of plywood and drag it home as if it were on a tobaggon. Dig a pit 4 ft. deep x 3 ft. x 3 ft. Get a bed of good hot coals about 6 to 8 inches deep in the pit, then shovel in 6 inches of sand. Drop deer in, cover with plastic sheet, and refill rest of hole with sand. Allow to cook for two days. Retrieve deer. Serves 58 diners with some tolerance for sand in their food.

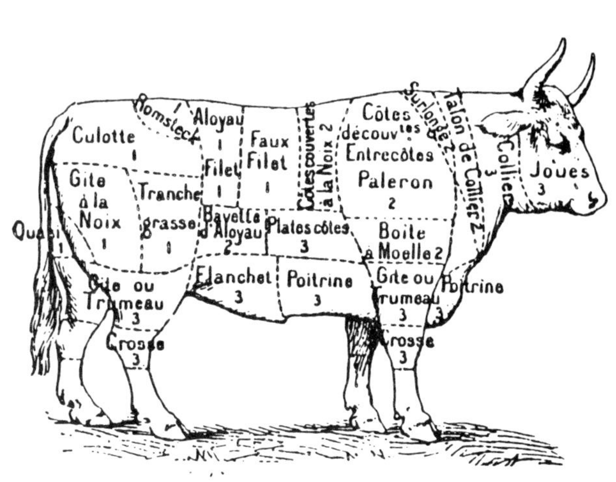
Culotte 1
Romsteck 1
Aloyau 1
Filet 1
Faux Filet 1
Côtes couvertes à la Noix 2
Côtes découvtes
Entrecôtes
Paleron 2
Surlonge 2
Talon de Collier 2
Collier 3
Joues 3
Gite à la Noix 1
Tranche grasse 1
Quasi 1
Bavette d'Aloyau 2
Plates côtes 3
Boite à Moelle 2
Gite ou Trumeau 3
Flanchet 3
Poitrine 3
Gite ou Trumeau 3
Poitrine 3
Crosse 3
Crosse 3

CHAPTER II

Personal preferences are your guide, of course, in terms of what kinds of animals you choose to harvest along our highways.

While most cooks are well aware of which animals are eatable and which are not, perhaps the following list will be useful to the neophyte *Ventre Montanter*.

I. **Gamebirds** of all descriptions. Common species are pheasant, quail, partridege, turkey and dove.

Aquatic birds such as ducks and geese are usually found in *Ventre Montant* form only on airstrips where the competition for airspace can get downright nasty.

Since *Ventre Montanters* have only infrequent access to airstrips, recipes for aquatic birds will find only modest inclusion in this book.

A tragic accident happened in '34 on an airstrip outside of Des Moines. Professor Hobbs was foraging for some goodies on the strip and failed to notice an oncoming twin engine. The authorities used Prof. Hobb's own shovel to gather the good man up.

(II) **Rabbits** in *Ventre Montant* form are unique in that they will invariably have a surprised look on their face. This is a bit odd since these are the very same critters that lurk along the sides of the road and in ditches just waiting for a car to run out in front of. It gives one reason to question the intelligence of those cute little furry things.

(III) **Squirrels** are an easy animal to spot while foraging. The *Ventre Montant* squirrels usually welcomes the intrepid forager with a cheerful wave of his tail as it blows in the passing breeze.

(IV) **Deer** are, of course, the forager's jackpots. The amount of meat that can be foraged is often sufficient for a family reunion, bridal shower, office party, or other such event.

While we would all like to think of *Ventre Montanters* as being men and women of honor, there is some evidence that one will, on occasion, deliberately run down a deer. This is a base and dastardly act, unbecoming either amateur or professional.

Scalloped Chipmonks

4-6 chipmonks
2 medium potatoes
1 medium onion
1 C. milk
1 pkg. cream of onion soup
Poultry seasoning, to taste
Salt and pepper

Slice potatoes and onions. Lay chipmunk fragments on top. Add milk and dried soup. Top off with seasoning, to taste. Bake at 375° for 1½ hours. Serves 6.

(V) **Coon** are often found in groups as they are naturally gregarious and tend to place undue confidence in the leadership abilities of any one of them who will, often inadvisably, cross a road.

(VI) **Opposum** is an animal commonly used for food in the southern portion of Iowa. Delicious dishes can be made of this nocturnal animal and the reader is urged to consider the recipes in this book.

(VIII) **Turtles** are logical candidates for the art of *Ventre Montant* cooking as they are slow of foot and have limited cerebral skills. The reader, should refer to the recipe for Turtles on the Half Shell.

(IX) **Crawfish** make for excellent foraging. Unfortunately, their size often prevents one from getting enough of them at one time for a full recipe. It is often preferred to mix them with the insects from your car radiator into a rich thick puree. Olive oil is sometimes added for smoothness.

(X) **Chickens** are often found on the road near houses that are close by the road. Recipes found in "straight" cookbooks can be referred to for preparing tasty dishes of these luckless layers.

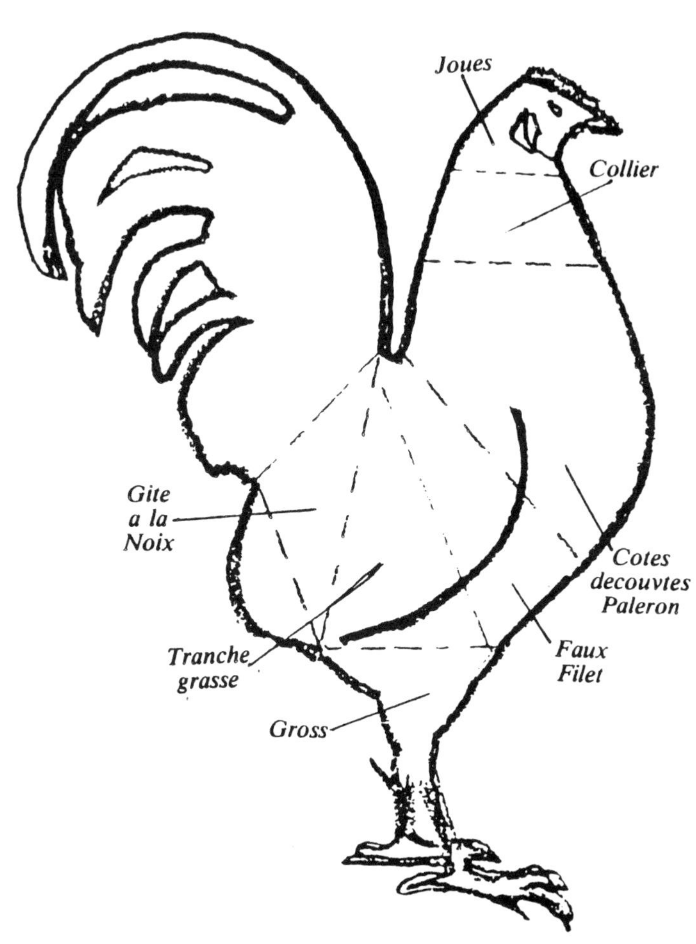
Joues
Collier
Gite
a la
Noix
Cotes
decouvtes
Paleron
Tranche
grasse
Faux
Filet
Gross

CHAPTER III

Like most areas of human endeavor, there are proper methods of gathering expired critters along the road, and there are improper ones. One should be most careful in observing the rules of etiquette. While this volume cannot cover, in detail, all the rules, some general guidelines follow:

(1) He who finds first, gets.

(2) Leave some for seed. If, for example, we removed every dead animal from the road, what whould attract the crows? Were we to be that foolish, we would find that dead crows would be virtually unobtainable.

(3) Leave the area at least as neat as you find

it. If, for example, a tail or a leg falls off a "find", pick it up and take it with you, or throw it in the ditch before you leave.

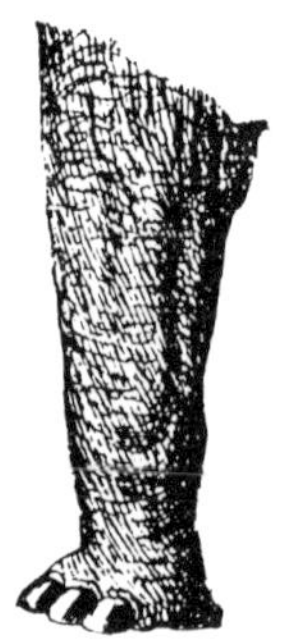

Remember: Above all, Safety First. One can, himself, become the victim of oncoming traffic. Many of us recall with sadness the case of Wilber Eddington of near Deep River who had gotten out of his car to gather up a female racoon that had cashed in her chips on Highway #21 out of Deep River. Right behind the mother racoon were three little ones, all in a a row, all probably hit by the same vehicle. Wilbert was standing there on the highway considering the irony of those little bandits that had trustingly followed their mother to her death there on the road.

Wilbert was as kind-hearted a man as any. He scooped up a pile of fur and was undoubtedly saddened by what he saw. His attention was probably diverted by his charitable thoughts when that "eighteen wheeler" came along. That truck faltened Wilbert right there. When they found him the next morning, he was stretched out right between the second and third baby coon, right in a row with the rest of them.

GOOSEBERRY STUFFED CHICKEN

¼ C. gooseberries
½ C. bread crumbs or crackers
1 pkg. dried onion soup
¼ lb. butter
1 tsp. salt
½ tsp. pepper
1 Ventre Montant chicken

Mix gooseberries, crumbs (or crackers), soup, and butter. Insert in chicken, perferably after removal of innards. Bake at 375° for 2½ hours. Sprinkle with salt and pepper; then bake another 15 minutes.

CHAPTER IV

Now, there is just no point in accepting the commonly held belief here in Iowa that folks who partake of fallen fauna are any less fastidious than anyone else. That just isn't true. It would behoove all of us who practice *Ventre Montant* cooking to do what we can to stop those ugly rumors.

There are three kinds of vittles out there along the yellow stripes. One is fresh, one is ripe, and the third has been around long enough to be dessicated, or Seche as the French prefer to call it.

Folks who salvage our furred and feathered friends use that which is either fresh or "Seche", just like anyone else. Have you ever priced dried meat at the gourmet section of your local grocery store? If so, you know that Seche comes dear.

Of course, we who are adventurous enough to eat

the products of *Ventre Montant* do find it necessary to establish which of the three degrees of freshness a particular "find" will fall into.

One should be careful not to get into the habit of simply walking up to the critter and giving it a good swift kick in the Solar Plexus. That can result in a real problem that's not a whole lot of fun to have. The reader is urged to refer to page 51 regarding methods of deflating a rotund critter. Far better to be safe than sorry.

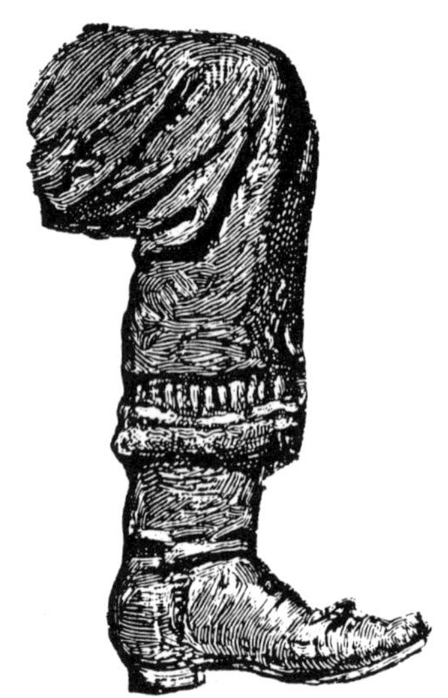

A far better and wiser way is to approach the critter from downward. Unless you have a bad head cold this is as good a way as any of establishing if the critter has progressed to the point of being ripe or not.

If and after one determines if the critter is fresh, ripe, or Seche, he can then approach it quite boldly if that determination has shown it to be fresh or Seche.

Very often if it is found to be dessicated, it will have been on the road long enough to be flattened. If fact, judicious observation in the field will reveal that skunks, coon, squirrels, and rabbits can be reduced to being only about 0.75 inches tall within a very short time.

If the animal is dessicated, one will find it to be considerably lighter in weight than it would be otherwise. This can be of real importance if you happen to be a considerable distance from your vehicle or if you are on a date and don't want to work up a sweat.

If the animal is flattened, it will then also lend itself to being carried. The hearty *Ventre Montanter* will be able to carry a considerable number of such critters in a sturdy canvas bag.

OVEN BBQed PHEASANT

1 pheasant
1 T. brown sugar
2 T. vegetable oil
¼ C. Pepsi Cola
1 T. soy sauce
1 C. diced carrot
6 oz. marbleade
1 T. Real Lemon

Brown the pheasant in oil, make sauce from rest of ingredients. Bake pheasant for two hours at 400° covered with foil. On occasion, open foil and baste with sauce. Keep foil open the last 15 minutes of the two hours.

With a view toward etiquette, gastronomic courtesy compells us to recognize that *Ventre Montant* is that that happens only by accident. It is considered very unethical to deliberately run over a critter, then claim it to be *Ventre Montant*.

Likewise, the neighbor's pets such as his cats and dogs, no matter how much noise they cause at night, do not *Ventre Montant* make.

Sometimes difficulties in identification of an animal can unfortunately result in a cat ending up as the Soup of The Day since they can be confused with the highly edible young raccoon.

A *Ventre Montanter* of good taste will however, let that happen only indavertently.

MYSTERY TIDBITS

4 lbs. assorted meat of unknown identification
½ pt. soy sauce
Green olives

Cut meat into chunks about ½" square. Soak in soy sauce overnight. Sponge tidbits off with paper towel, and dry in oven at 275°.

Secure each tidbit on a toothpick along with a green olive. Serves 1 to 17 people.

THE ALL PURPOSE SUBSTITUTE

One very flat and dried (Seche) goat
Other ingredients as appropriate

This recipe is one that involves the substituting of a goat in place of anything you might be out of or would rather not use. For example, if the doctor has ordered you to use less salt, when you encounter a recipe that calls for salt, just use one goat instead. If you happen to be out of bay leaves and your veggie soup called for a bay leaf, just forget the bay leaf and pitch in a goat instead.

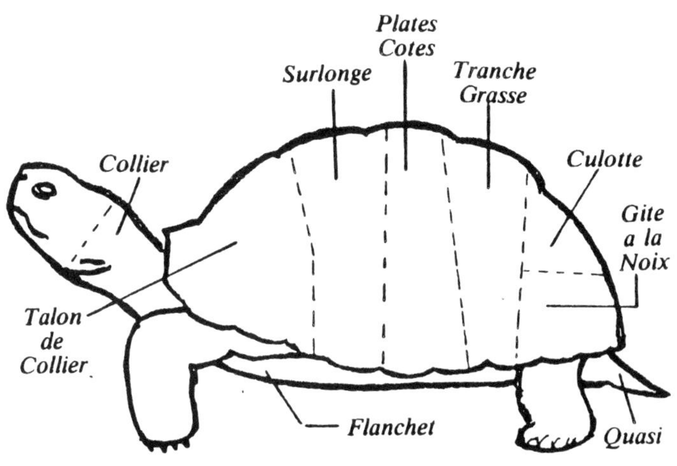
Plates
Cotes
Surlonge
Tranche
Grasse
Collier
Culotte
Gite
a la
Noix
Talon
de
Collier
Flanchet
Quasi

TURKEY SUPREME

1 Road Kilt Turkey
6 T. brown sugar
1 C. chopped onions
½ C. cooking oil
Salt
Pepper

Roast turkey for one hour at 400°, then make a paste of the sugar, the . . . . Oh, forget it. It's not that good anyway.

Large dead animals will usually be found lying on their side. On occasion, however, they will exhibit symptoms of morbidity usually common to small animals. Thus they will, sometimes, be found lying on their backs. This illustration shows a dead cow that died near Marshalltown on Highway 233.

CHAPTER V

It would be well for the careful forager to take a leaf from the notebooks of game hunters, and observe every precaution on approaching an animal that appears to have gone to that Great Rest Stop In The Sky.

Like game hunters, any *Ventre Montanter* who has been in the field very long will happen upon a critter who hasn't quite given up the ghost yet.

And anyone who thinks that a rabbit or a squirrel is much too cute to bite doesn't fully understand the nature of the beasts.

'POSSUM PARFAIT

Innerds from medium-sized opposum
¾ cup corn syrup
Dash salt
2 cups heavy cream

Heat syrup to 230 degrees. Pour over innerds while beating constantly. Beat 'til cool. Add salt. Fold in cream. Place in molds and freeze without stirring.

The amatuer forager will often approach the subject with a timid:

"Are you dead?"

The irrationality of such an act is too obvious to even warrent much comment. If it is dead, it can't answer. If it isn't dead, it won't answer.

It is far better to approach the animal while making a noise like an oncoming automobile. If the creature had had one unhappy experience with an automobile, it is likely going to do what it can to avoid a second one if it is still among the living.

Some of the less sporting among those who practice the gentle art of *Ventre Montanting* have been known to get back into the car and approach the animal whose expiration is yet questionable in order to elicit a "flight or fight" reaction.

You should be advised that such carryings-on are considered to be poor form. Happily we can rest assured that most animals seen lying along the road are thoroughly dead.

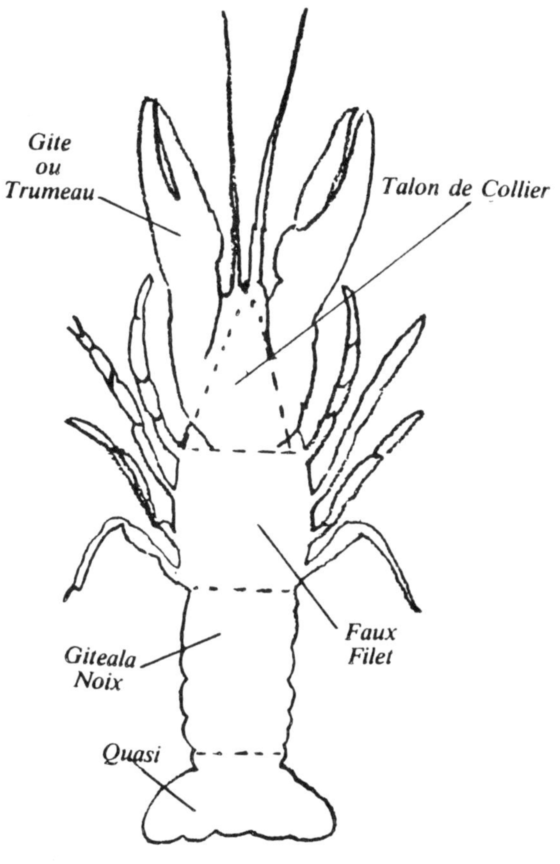
Gite
ou
Trumeau
Talon de Collier
Giteala
Noix
Faux
Filet
Quasi

CHAPTER VI

In this business of preparing gastronomic delights from traffic victims, we must be aware that time and temperature will sometimes take their toll on freshly flattened fatalities. In this volume we will refer to that as gaseous inflation rather than the less delicate phrase "all swoll up like a daid hog."

When one finds a critter that has all the appearance of a basketball with little short legs, one can assume he has a case of gaseus inflation on

his hands. Other possibilities are a critter with a real bad case of heartburn or even a basketball with real short legs. These, however, can be discounted pretty much off hand.

BAKED S– –E

This recipe is available only on a need-to-know basis. And, believe me, you wouldn't even want to know.

In such event, you simply have to face it. You have a case of " . . . . all swoll up like a . . . .", I mean Gaseous Inflation on your hands.

Under such circumstances one should avoid the obvious methods of correcting the situation such as sticking them with a knife or stompin' on 'em right there on the pavement.

Either of these techniques can make a fellow sure wish he had never found that particular critter.

Some *Ventre Montanter* enthusiasts purchase and use one of the many commerically available deflators.

Most people, however simply get back into the car and drive over the hapless critter again. It is often advisable to turn the car radio up loud while doing that. Also, one should avoid having someone stand outside the car to direct the driver in this operation. Such navigators tend to resist doing that a second time after they get splattered good.

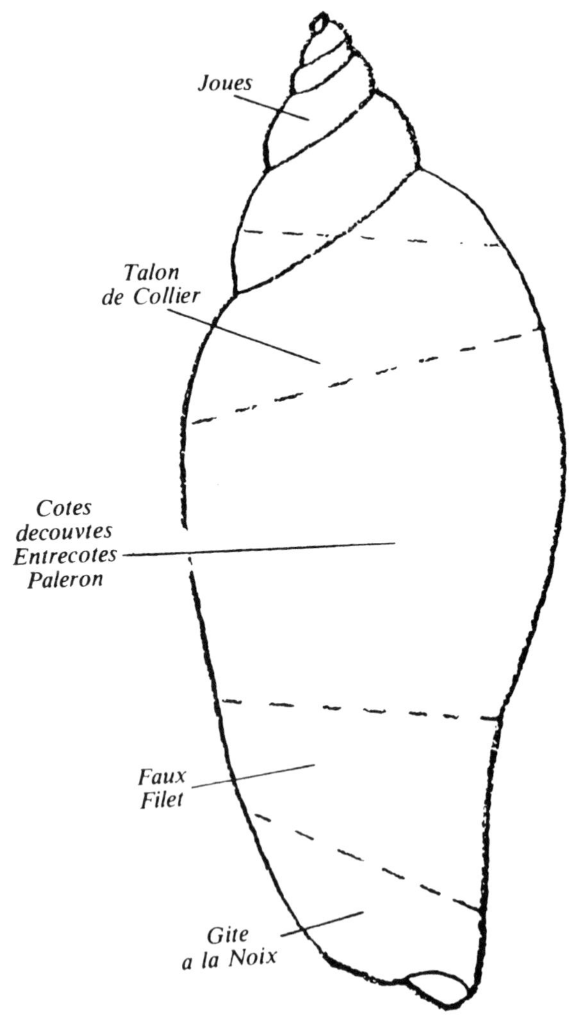
Joues
Talon
de Collier
Cotes
decouvtes
Entrecotes
Paleron
Faux
Filet
Gite
a la Noix

While this probably wouldn't qualify as a recipe, it might be of interest to our readers with pets to consider armadilo eggs as "gnaw" toys for their kitty or dog.

The fact that the egg might suddenly transform into a walking-way-type-armadillo adds a certain element of suspense to your pet's life that might be lacking now.

INTERSTATE POTLUCK

Here is an opportunity to put to good use all the parts, fragments, and unidentifiable hunks of whatever that tend to accumulate in the freezer.

4 lbs. assorted parts, cleaned of fur and feather as well as possible
4 tomatoes (average size)
2 green peppers
1 tsp. salt
¼ tsp. pepper

Combine assorted parts, tomatoes, and pepper in a stew pot. Add water, and boil until the toughest part is edible or until pot burns through. Season with salt and pepper, to taste. Serves eight.

INSTANT JERKY

1 medium squirrel (dried)
6 oz. soy sauce
1 tsp. pepper
½ tsp. dried onions

Mix the soy sauce, pepper, and dried onions. Heat to boiling, then cool. Soak squirrel in above overnight in foil covered dish. Remove squirrel, dry with towel, warm in oven to crisp. Makes excellent jerky.

CHAPTER VII

This cookbook recognizes that carcasses gathered from the field for *Ventre Montant* cookery will oft times be found when the shapes are considerably different than most members of the species.

For example, pheasants are normally of the nature of a lumpy football. In the world of road kills, however, pheasants are more often shaped like a pizza or the little balls of dust that gather under beds. The recipes in this book are designed to take that situation into account. It is, therefore, not necessary to "fluff" a creature back into its original shape.

In fact the misshappened nature of many of the "finds" one can come across offers opportunities not offered by "straight" cooking. It gives you the chance to do some creative species transfers.

John Scone from up by Sac City, for example, was real partial to quail but was rarely able to find any of those delicious little birds. He did, however, often find a smacked deer along Highway #175.

SQUIRREL SURPRISE

One squirrel
4 T. cooking oil
Salt
Pepper

Preheat frying pan to a temperature that will tend to char any residues from previous meal. Put oil in pan, and add squirrel with hide intact. Fry 'til tender to a fork. Remove squirrel. The hair will stick to pan, thereby releasing the squirrel. This procedure enables one to avoid the messy job of removing the hide prior to cooking.

John didn't particularly care for venison, so he'd let his finds age just enough that they would be plenty pliable. Then he'd grind those deer up and sort of knead 'em into the shape of quail. John would fill his freezer with those cloven-hoofed quail and enjoy them year around.

John's little habit got him out of a nasty confrontation with the game warden in Sac County one day. The good officer got wind of John having a whole freezer full of quail and got himself a search warrant to see for himself. He wasn't about to let anyone in the county get away with such a flagrant violation of the law.

Well, it was a real mess. The warden found a whole bunch of those "quail", but also found out they were made out of venison. In the confusion over the species, John got off scot-free. They had him charged with an illegal deer for a while, then they changed it to illegal quail. Then they switched back again. By the time the whole thing was settled, John didn't have to pay any fine at all.

FAMILY FAVORITE CIVIT KABOBS

1 medium-sized civit cat
2 lbs. spiced road apples
½ lb. hedgeball slices, quartered
6 ozs. mushrooms
½ C. extra hot ketchup

½ C. bittersweet marmalade
2 T. finely chopped onions
2 T. liquid dish soap

(Continued on Next Page)

(Family Favorite Civit Kabobs)

(Continued)

1 T. prune juice
1 to 1½ tsp. dry mustard

Stick the civit cat fragments, road apples, hedgeball slices, and mushrooms alternately on skewers. For sauce, combine remaining ingredients. Broil civit cat and fruit over slow coals 12 to 15 minutes; brush often with sauce.

Use rotating skewers or turn skewers frequently during broiling. Serves 4.

CRUNCHY COON GIZZARDS

COMBINE:
2 C. coon innerds
1 C. rye flour
2 duck eggs (if unavailable, use chicken eggs)
2 C. Rice Krispies

Spread in greased 9 x 13-inch pan. Bake at 350° for 45 minutes.

FROSTING:
1 C. chopped coon gizzards
5 large Hershey bars

Mix in blender until smooth. Spread on baked innards and season to taste. Serves 4.

CHAPTER VIII

hile the provious chapter offered assurances that it was not necessary to “fluff’ an animal back to its original shape, this book also recognizes that some people do want the critter they eat to look like they did when they were frolicing around in the wild.

The following three techinques are offered as means of restoring a creature to an approximation of its original size.

I. **THE PETRIR METHOD**

“Petrir” is French for “to knead” so it is rether self-explanatory. The carcass is simply kneaded back into shape by manual manipulation. The kneader will often find that presoaking in water or vegetable oil will facilitate this.

The reader is warned that he runs a reasonable risk of ant bites while doing this. A box of baking soda kept handy to treat these ant bites can be useful.

(II) LE METHODE' GONFLEMENT

This method is often used in the summertime when firecrackers are available. It simply involves inserting the firecracker into the animal and igniting it. The resulting explosion serves to reinflate the critter. The results are fast but unpredictable. It is a technique often used on birds. The little pieces of paper from the firecracker often go unnoticed when used on birds as they are so similar to feather fragments that they often go unseen by even the discriminating diner.

A variation of *Le Methode' Gonflement* is the ignition of the flammable methane gas inside the animal that results from the natural aging process in the hot sun. This too, in fact, can be a bit on the messy side. Knowledgeable *Gonflementers* tend to either hide behind trees or use Methods I or III.

(III) THE 90 DEGREE TURN TECHNIQUE

This method is often effective unless the critter has become flattened too much. The procedure is fairly straightforward. One simply places the slightly flattened animal on edge and runs over it again with an automobile. It will more or less undo what the original vehicle already did.

CRITTERS ALONG THE ROAD

When ya spot them critters along the road, and yur shore that they're quite daid; Scoop 'em up 'til you got a load. Take 'em home and put on a spread.

FROG CHIPS

12 small to medium-sized flattened frogs
1 C. peanut oil
Salt

Heat frogs in 300° oven 'til crispy. Soak in oil for 2 hours. Sponge dry; add salt and reheat for one more hour. Break into potato-sized chips and serve with any conventional dip.

CHAPTER IX

The art of *Ventre Montant* is not insensitive to the march of progress. Just as the wood stove, then the gas, then the electric, the crock pot, the mixer, and the microwave all had their influences, so do the circumstances inherent in road kills.

Factors that influences cooking times for instance, are such tings as the temperature and mechanical influences to which the critter has been subjected. All the recipes should be adjusted in terms of heating temperatures or time to allow for prolonged exposure to warm conditions.

If one is preparing a rabbit, for example, and the unfortunate creature was exposed to temperatures of 100° F. for several days, one must make appropriate adjustments. A rule of thumb to follow is 20° F. less or ½ hour less cooking time for every day the bunny was exposed to temperatures of 100° F. out there on the road. Some practice might be necessary to perfect this fine tuning.

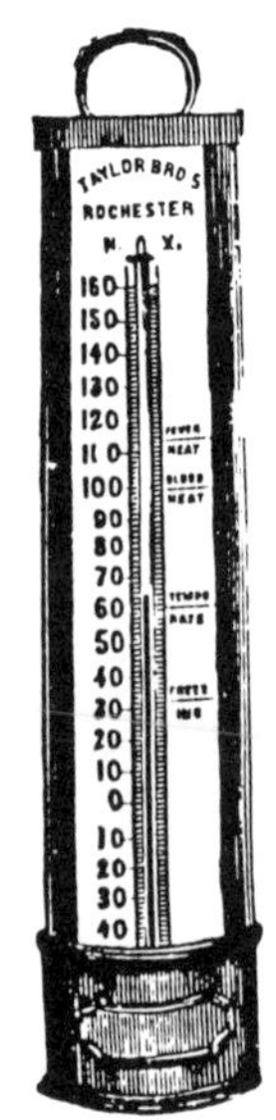

Also, since it is often difficult to determine how long a critter has laid on the concrete, the following guide can be useful:

0-1 day Hair or feathers remain unmatted or even glisten with the gloss of live and healthy animal.

2-3 days Hair of features become dull and lifeless. It may even become badly matted. Extremities such as feet, ears, beaks, and tails have a dehydrated appearance. Swelling may be apparent.

4-6 days Any earlier distending of the creature has subsided. The muscles have become quite rigid.

7-14 days Small animals tend to be no taller than ¼ to ½ inch and dessicated. Very often one finds it best, at this point, to forget recipes and simply use the creature as a frisbee. These animals are often called "sailers" as they will sail very well when thrown as a frisbee. The reader should be cautioned that state laws very widely in regard to sailing dead animals on or near a highway.

Large animals aged to this extend have been known to cause foragers to forget the whole enterprise and to take up some other course of study.

In addition to the effects of temperature, one should take into consideration the tenderizing effects on an animal of being repeatedly run over.

Wintertime foraging is perfectly permissable, but one should, as in any other case, allow for effects of freezing and other environmental considerations.

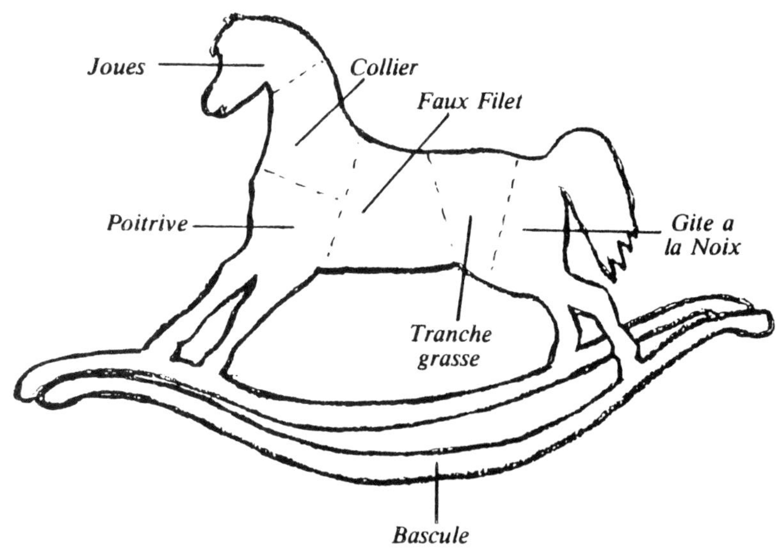
Joues
Collier
Faux Filet
Poitrive
Gite a
la Noix
Tranche
grasse
Bascule

CHAPTER X

Sometimes *Ventre Montant* can be a means of accomplishing desirable social goods far beyond simply providing a meal or two.

It was in the fall of '63 when Leonard Moorlan was grappling with the biggest decision of his life. He was on the verge of quitting his job as a rural mail carrier and risking his entire life savings. Leonard wanted to go into the business of molding musical instrument parts in plastic. He felt he could do it and make good money at it.

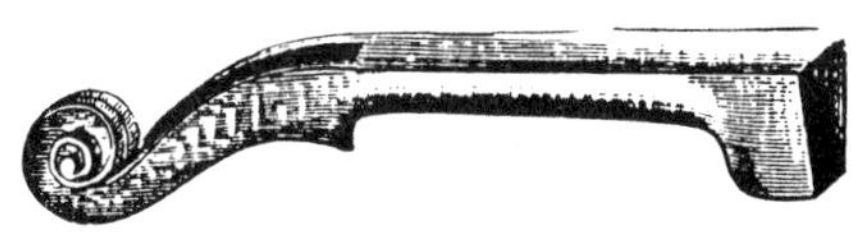

The problem was his indecisiveness on the issue. He felt that if he took the plunge, he would either become rich or stone broke. It was a hard decision. He had the money and was still young enough to make it work if anyone could. He had taken a series of classes at the University of Idaho in Iowa City and felt he had the knowhow. It was just a matter of working up the courage to do it.

Leonard was driving down Highway #20 one night he felt that he simply had to make a decision that night. He could no longer put it off.

Leonard was really agonizing over the whole thing, afraid not to do it, yet also afraid that if he did he might end up starving.

His answer was to watch the road particularly carefully that night. He decided that if he saw a lot of groceries he'd take that as a sign that a life of plenty awaited him in the plastics molding business. If, however, he saw little or none he'd take that as a sign that he would do poorly in any molding venture.

Fate works in strange ways for sure. It wasn't but a part of a minute later that he saw a coon on the road. Within a minute or two later, he spied two rabbits. Already, Leonard was feeling good about his decision to leave the issue upto fate. Things were already looking favorable for him, what with seeing that coon plus two rabbits.

About three miles down the road, however, a drama was being played out that was going to affect Leonard dramatically. A sleepy truckdriver miscalculated that cure on Highway #20 just north of Early. His load of hogs tipped and fell over.

Those poor hogs were buffeted around inside that truck like they had never been before.

Between the impact of the truck hitting the side of the ditch and the poor critters desperate attempts to escape, many of those hogs died right there at the curve.

Within seconds the highway was strewn with the carcasses of what would have been fine hams and bacon had that driver been a bit more alert. A local farmer who heard the commotion and came to help told later that a man could have crossed from one side of the highway to the other and the backs of those hogs and never once would have had to step down on the pavement.

COLD CROW CUTS

One medium to large crow
Chicken broth
Poultry seasoning
Salt and pepper

Clean the crow, as well as reasonable of feathers and gravel. Boil crow for 20 minutes. Remove meat from bones and grind meat. Boil again for 10 minutes in the broth, add ¼ teaspoon of poultry seasoning and salt and pepper. Set aside and allow to set up. Slice with sharp knife and use as sandwich meat or appetizers.

Well, anyway, along comes Leonard, immersed in his thoughts of a career in plastics molding.

One can only imagine what Leonard thought when he saw that fate had provided an answer in no uncertain terms. He had never seen so much *Ventre Montant* in his life, and all in one place. Leonard had to bring his car to a complete stop to avoid running into all those dead hogs.

Leonard Moorlan made his decision right there on

the spot. Without even bothering to salvage any of those hogs, Leonard rushed right home to share the excitement of his decision with his wife. He was going to do it! He was going to get into the plastics molding business and mold parts for musical instruments!

Today the Moorlan plastic rain gauges and measuring cups are shipped to points throughout the entire upper Midwest. Though he never did mold any parts for musical instruments, his Cler-Vue rain gauges and his Ever-Accurate measuring cups are tributes to the courage of a man who recognized the meaning of a highway full of dead hogs.

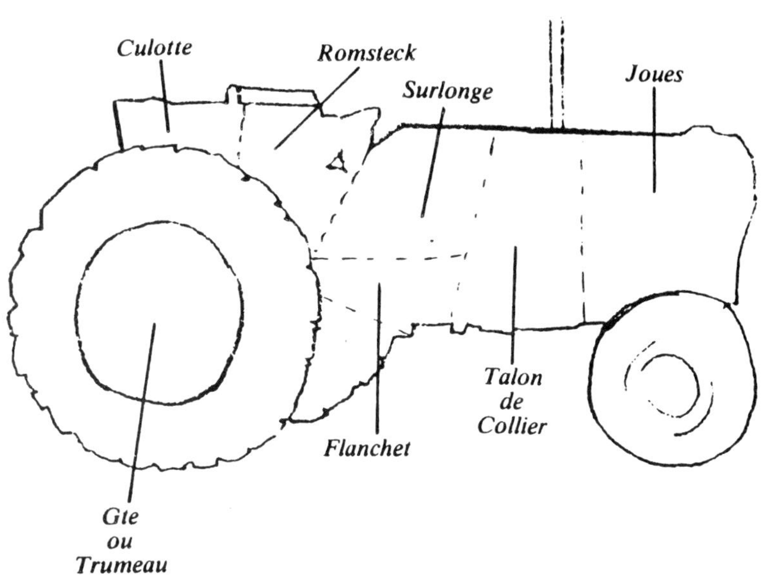
Culotte
Romsteck
Surlonge
Joues
Talon
de
Collier
Flanchet
Gte
ou
Trumeau

CHAPTER XI

Speaking of tenderizing stuff, young Gary McFadden of over near Centerville suffered through an embarassing summer back in '22.

Gary was cutting along Highway 34 between Centerville and Bloomfield when he spied what appeared to be a fine young chicken sprawled out there on the pavement. It looked like the bird had just raised his head up to catch an oil pan goin' down the highway long about 65 or 70 miles an hour.

Some other chickens there from the neighboring farmhouse were, in fact, still messing around there along the shoulder of the highway, pickin' up some corn spilled by a grain truck.

Well, now. Gary wasn't one to let such a prize go to someone else, so he skidded his car to a stop, snatched up that hapless hen and continued on toward home.

When Gary got back to the house, he took that chicken in to show to his mother. Mrs. McFadden was more than glad to see that nice chicken so she set about to fix it for the following day's dinner. In her eagerness to get that chicken goin' she didn't take the time to examine it well like she should have. That little molded-in label under the fowl's beak that said "Flexible Theatrical Products Company" would have been her first clue that she didn't have a real chicken at all. It was nothing but a rubber chicken lost along the road from a car-top carrier of a traveling bunch of vaudeville actors. Unfortunately, that little message under the beast's beak escaped her notice.

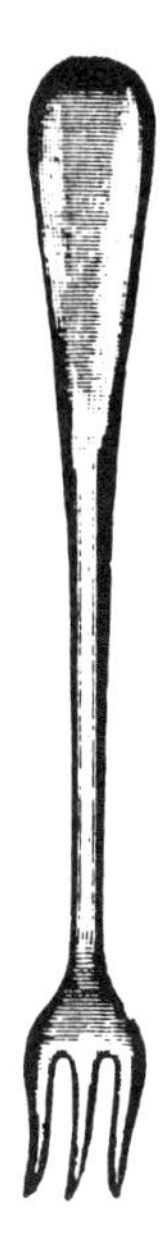

Mrs. McFadden had a time-tested method for determining just how tough a chicken was going to prove to be. It involved sticking a pickle fork in 'em and giving it a twist. The way the fork would return to the original position was her clue to how tough the bird was and how long she would have to cook it. She pulled that little test on Gary's find and was shocked to see that fork bounce back like it was spring loaded.

Mrs. McFadden knew right then that she had a mighty tough customer on her hands, so she got out the old trusty tenderizer and beat around on that critter for a minute or two with it.

That rubber chicken proved to be unaffected by the tenderizing process because second test result was the same as before.

Now, Mrs. McFadden wasn't about to let a little old road-kilt chicken get the best of her so she moved up to the four-pound chicken tenderizer. Raising that thing up the air over her head, she beat around on that chicken with a real vengeance. It was something to behold!

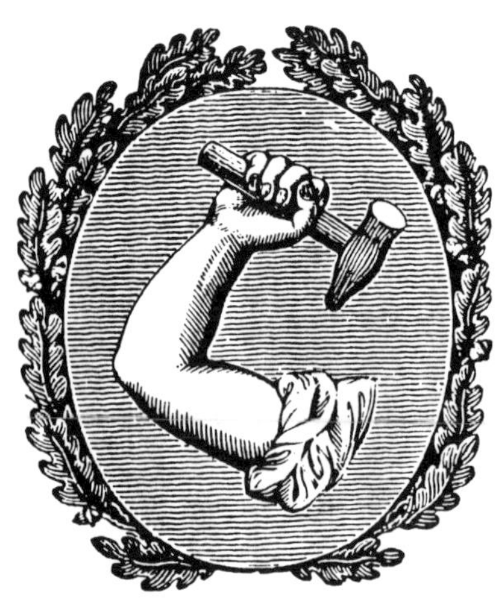

Even a rubber chicken is not totally unaffected by the McFadden tenderizer. The repeated pounding on that hunk of rubber just sort of took the starch right out of it enough that Mrs. McFadden was convinced that she had the job done well enough.

Just to be sure she got the last vestige of toughness out of that surprisingly tough chicken, Mrs. McFadden soaked it overnight in battery acid, then in some 1918 Broudeax for a couple of hours just prior to cooking it.

A fellow has to conceed that a rubber chicken leads a pretty rough life. They get sat on, stretched out of shape, and used to backhand a straight man. Few of the rubber chickens from Fexible Theatrical Products Company had, however, to go through what Gary's did. All that pounding around and soaking actually did tenderize that bird enough that the family had a nice dinner the next day.

It was after dinner when the folks were settin' around the table just talking when Gary's little sister, Irene, idly turned over a small piece of what was left of that chicken there on her plate. At first she didn't quite know what to make of what she saw. She was mystified to see what looked like a label of some sort on the chicken.

Well, you guessed it. Irene had the neck piece and it still had that little molded-in label there on her plate. There it set, big as life: *Flexible Theatrical Products Company*.

The family soon discovered that they had eaten a honest-to-goodness rubber chicken.

It wouldn't have been too bad if it was let drop right there, but no such luck. Irene had to tell her whole fourth-grade class about it the next day.

It was a good long time 'til Gary McFadden heard the last of his rubber chicken that he had thought was a simple piece of *Ventre Montant*

CHAPTER XII

Surprise! Surprise! This last story in the book isn't about *Ventre Montant* at all. It has nothing to do with it. I'm including it in this book, though, because it's a good story and I like it. If you don't like it you'll simply have to put up with it. Besides, I've already gotten your money anyway.

This tale was told to me by my friend, John Gorham who was one of twelve children back on the farm. John has long left the farm, being a photographer and all, now. The scars of being one of a large family back in the thirties and fourties remain, however.

It seems that one day when John was a boy, the family

was having some company for supper.

Mrs. Gorham found herself caugh a mite shy on groceries, so she took John and his brother Wilber, aside.

"Now, boys, we don't have enough meat for everybody, so when it comes around you two gotta say you don't want any."

With some grumbling, the pair agreed. It was generally understood that it wasn't in a person's best interest to disagree with Mrs. Gorham.

The hour arrived and everybody sat down; that large family plus the company. Things were just as planned. The food was passed, and each helped himself to a nice generous helping of meat. Everybody, that is, except John and Wilber. That forbidden fruit first came to Wilber. He tried not to inhale for fear of getting a whiff of that beautiful roast. He quite casually suggested that he didn't care for any. For one wild moment, he toyed with the idea of spearing a nice hunk of that roast, but he knew better. He could feel his mother's eyes focused right on him. Nonchalantly he passed that plate on to John just as if all it had on it were some carrot sticks.

John glanced idly at the plate and passed it on to yet another brother. Quite coolheaded he was about it all. Not so his stomach. It was frantically yelling to his head to have John drop that nice big piece on the edge off onto his plate. That was to no avail. John had felt the sting of his mother's wrath enough times to know better.

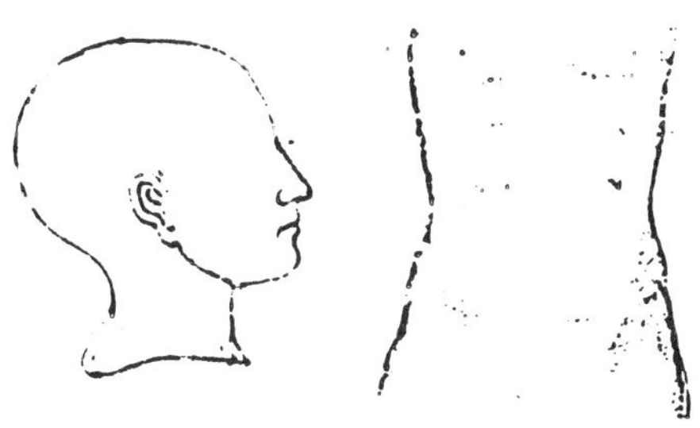

Apparently the boys pulled it off quite well. The meal went without a hitch. Those two boys had some difficulty whipping up a lot of interest in the small talk so typical of mealtime down on the farm. They would have liked to made up for the lack of any meat by wolfing down a mite heavier on the 'taters and gravy. But they didn't. They had been duly warned about that, too.

Soon it was time to clear off the table. Mrs. Gorham quickly did that to make way for the dessert. This hadn't been mentioned, so the boys kind of perked up when they heard their mother getting down those familiar sherbet glasses.

The pair held a whispered conference there at the end of the table, speculating as to what might be forthcoming. The two had spent a long day working on fixin' their father's windmill and they were still hungry.

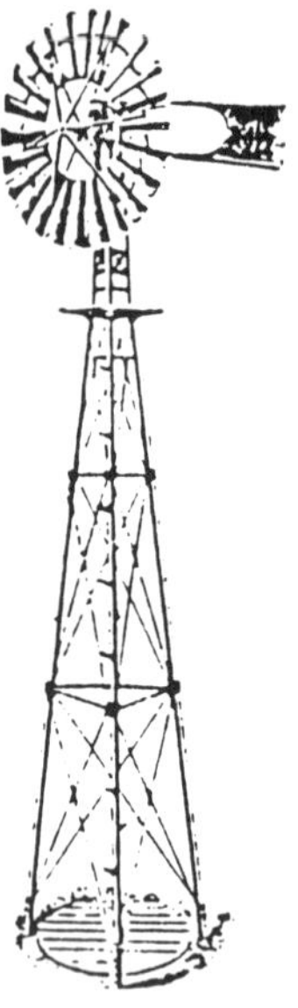

Dessert was always a joyous occasion, but dessert after that meal was nothing less than a Godsend. For what seemed like an eternity, the hungry pair waited for their mother's return.

Sure enough, in a few minutes, Mrs. Gorham came back to the dining room bearing a large tray with a multitude of sherbet glasses, each filled with a strawberry concoction. The boys saw those big beautiful berries fattened against the inside of the glass, all covered with a mound of homemade whipped cream. On top of each scoop of that whipped cream sat another huge berry in solitary splendor. That couldn't have been a more welcome sight to John and Wilber. It was as if everything was all right with the world again.

As Mrs. Gorham returned to the dining room with that treasure, she solved another problem that she hadn't told her sons about. Her problem was that she was a bit shy of dessert, also. Her solution was to enter the room with the following announcement:

"Well, here's some dessert. But anyone who didn't eat their meat doesn't get any."

NEED A GIFT?

For

• Shower • Birthday • Mother's Day •
• Anniversary • Christmas •

Turn Page For Order Form

(Order NOW While Supply Lasts!)

TO ORDER COPIES OF

IOWA'S ROAD KILL COOKBOOK

Please send me _______ copies of **Iowa's Road Kill Cookbook** at $7.95 each. (Make checks payable to **QUIXOTE PRESS.**)

Name ________________________________

Street ________________________________

City________________State____________Zip Code______

SEND ORDERS TO:
QUIXOTE PRESS

R.R. #4, Box 33B • Blvd. Station
Sioux City, Iowa 51109

TO ORDER COPIES OF

IOWA'S ROAD KILL COOKBOOK

Please send me _______ copies of **Iowa's Road Kill Cookbook** at $7.95 each. (Make checks payable to **QUIXOTE PRESS.**)

Name ________________________________

Street ________________________________

City________________State____________Zip Code______

SEND ORDERS TO:
QUIXOTE PRESS

R.R. #4, Box 33B • Blvd. Station
Sioux City, Iowa 51109

If you have enjoyed this book, perhaps you would enjoy others from Quixote Press.

GHOSTS OF THE MISSISSIPPI RIVER
Mpls. to Dubuque by Bruce Carlson .....paperback $9.95

GHOSTS OF THE MISSISSIPPI RIVER
Dubuque to Keokuk by Bruce Carlson....paperback $9.95

GHOSTS OF THE MISSISSIPPI RIVER
Keokuk to St. Louis by Bruce Carlson....paperback $9.95

GHOSTS OF JOHNSON COUNTY, IOWA
by Lori Erickson ....hardback $12.95

GHOSTS OF LINN COUNTY, IOWA
by Lori Erickson ....hardback $12.95

GHOSTS OF LEE COUNTY, IOWA
by Bruce Carlson ....hardback $12.00

GHOSTS OF DES MOINES COUNTY, IOWA
by Bruce Carlson ....hardback $12.00

GHOSTS OF SCOTT COUNTY, IOWA
by Bruce Carlson ....hardback $12.95

GHOSTS OF ROCK ISLAND COUNTY, ILLINOIS
by Bruce Carlson ....hardback $12.95

GHOSTS OF THE AMANA COLONIES
by Lori Erickson ....paperback $9.95

GHOSTS OF NORTHEAST IOWA
by Ruth Hein and Vicky Hinsenbrock....paperback $9.95

GHOSTS OF POLK COUNTY, IOWA
by Tom Welch ....paperback $9.95

GHOSTS OF THE IOWA GREAT LAKES
by Bruce Carlson ....paperback $9.95

(Continued on Next Page)

MISSISSIPPI RIVER PO' FOLK
by Pat Wallace .... paperback $9.95

STRANGE FOLKS ALONG THE MISSISSIPPI
by Pat Wallace .... paperback $9.95

THE VANISHING OUTHOUSE OF IOWA
by Bruce Carlson .... paperback $9.95

THE VANISHING OUTHOUSE OF ILLINOIS
by Bruce Carlson .... paperback $9.95

THE VANISHING OUTHOUSE OF MINNESOTA
by Bruce Carlson .... paperback $9.95

THE VANISHING OUTHOUSE OF WISCONSIN
by Bruce Carlson .... paperback $9.95

MISSISSIPPI RIVER COOKIN' BOOK
by Bruce Carlson .... paperback $11.95

IOWA'S ROAD KILL COOKBOOK
by Bruce Carlson .... paperback $7.95

HITCH HIKING THE UPPER MIDWEST
by Bruce Carlson .... paperback $7.95

IOWA, THE LAND BETWEEN THE VOWELS
by Bruce Carlson .... paperback $9.95

GHOSTS OF SOUTHWEST MINNESOTA
by Ruth Hein .... paperback $9.95

GHOSTS OF THE COAST OF MAINE
by Carole Olivieri Schulte .... paperback $9.95

ME 'N WESLEY
by Bruce Carlson .... paperback $9.95

INDEX

Index

...... Oh, what the heck. You don't really need an index for this book. Compiling an index can really be a pain in the neck and I'm not sure I'm up to it this morning.

Thanks for buying this book!